TEACHING OLD LOGS NEW TRICKS

MORE ABSURDITIES AND REALITIES OF EDUCATION

Cartoons by Michael F. Giangreco
Illustrations by Kevin Ruelle

Peytral Publications, Inc.
Minnetonka, MN 55345
952-949-8707

Copyright © 2000 by Michael F. Giangreco
First Printing 2000
Second Printing 2002

Publisher's Cataloguing-in-Publication
(Provided by Quality Books, Inc.)

Giangreco, Michael F. 1956-
    Teaching old logs new tricks ; more absurdities
and realities of education / cartoons by Michael
F. Giangreco ; illustrations by Kevin Ruelle. –
1 st ed.
    p. cm.
    ISBN: 1-890455-43-1

    1.   Education--Caricatures and cartoons.
2. Education--Humor.   I. Title.

    LA21.G52 2000   370.222
                        QBI00-438

    Library of Congress Catalog Card Number: 00-133655

Cartoon illustrations by Kevin Ruelle
Printed in the United States of America

Peytral Publications, Inc.
PO Box 1162
Minnetonka, MN 55345
952-949-8707
www.peytral.com

ii

Contents

About the Author

Michael F. Giangreco, Ph.D., is a Research Associate Professor at the University of Vermont (UVM). His work as a faculty member at UVM since 1988 has been on various projects with colleagues at the Center on Disability and Community Inclusion (the University Affiliated Program of Vermont) in the College of Education and Social Services. Since 1975 he has worked with children and adults with and without disabilities in a variety of capacities including camp counselor, community residence counselor, special education teacher, special education coordinator, educational consultant, university teacher, and researcher. Since 1982 he has written a number of traditional research studies, book chapters, and books. In 1998 Michael completed his first book of cartoons, *Ants in His Pants: Absurdities and Realities of Special Education.* This was followed in 1999 with the publication of *Flying by the Seat of Your Pants: More Absurdities and Realities of Special Education,* a second set of cartoons. Although he will continue his more traditional writing, he also plans to continue to infuse humor into his work and find creative ways to share information about the serious issues facing people with disabilities, their families, teachers, and service providers.

About the Illustrator

Kevin Ruelle has been an illustrator in Vermont for over twenty years. Cartoons are just one of the many applications of illustration that Kevin uses in his work. He runs a successful commercial art business, Ruelle Design and Illustration, located in Williston, Vermont. He and his associates produce all forms of visual communication and multimedia projects. Kevin lives with his wife, Neidi, and their four children in West Bolton, Vermont.

A Word from the Author

Teaching Old Logs New Tricks: More Absurdities and Realities of Education, is the third book of cartoons I have created with the invaluable assistance of my friend, artist Kevin Ruelle. If you have seen either of the first two books, *Ants in His Pants... or Flying by the Seat of Your Pants...,* you may already know how this collaboration between Kevin and me works. I create the original ideas, text, and sketches for each cartoon. But since my drawing abilities have been stalled at an early third-grade level, ever since I was in third-grade (that was in 1963), Kevin redraws my sketches. Then we edit them until they closely reflect the ideas represented in my original sketches.

In this book, I have maintained a focus on many of the themes that were included in the earlier books and have expanded the scope of topics. In *Teaching Old Logs New Tricks* you'll find cartoons on a variety of contemporary educational topics. Here are just some of them:

- Inclusive Education
- Teachers and Teaching
- Change
- Self-Advocacy
- Paraprofessionals
- Families
- Positive Behavior Support
- Disability Labeling
- Collaboration
- Special Education
- Support Services
- Least Restrictive Environment
- Supported Employment
- Individual Education Programs

As the author of several more traditional articles in professional journals and books, I have been pleasantly amazed by the power of cartoons to inform, encourage dialogue, spur action to improve education, and reduce stress by helping people smile. I have been equally intrigued by how different people respond to different cartoons. Everyone seems to have different favorites depending on their own experiences and sense of humor.

Cartoons from the early books have found their way on to the pages of a few books and many regional newsletters disseminated by schools, parent groups, disability advocacy organizations, and professional associations. The cartoons have been used extensively as overhead projections or within learning activities in undergraduate and graduate classes, at conferences, in workshops, and at other meetings. Parents have told me they have framed cartoons that closely reflected their own experiences and hung them in their homes or offices. Other parents have used them in meetings with professionals to help get their points across. They have been given as gifts to people who "get it" and handed out as door prizes. The Vermont Coalition for Disability Rights used them as part of "Disability Awareness Day" at the Vermont legislature. The cartoons can be used in innumerable creative ways.

Knowing that some of you will not have seen the previous two books of cartoons, I decided to repeat some of what I wrote before to ensure that readers have a clear understanding of my underlying thoughts and values in developing these cartoons. First, I value humor and think it is vital to our health, well-being, and creativity. Humor can also be a powerful learning tool. I wanted to address some of the serious issues of special and general education by poking fun at what we (people in the field) do. I have been challenged by the concern that some people might be offended by content that may hit a little too close to home. I have decided to take the chance that people in our field have a sufficient sense of humor to reflect on the satirical aspects of these cartoons, see the humor in them, and use them to promote better schooling. Friends and colleagues have warned me that my cartoons could be misused to promote practices that are the antithesis of what I have worked for my entire professional career. Just so there is no misunderstanding about what these cartoons stand for, I have listed here some of my beliefs related to the cartoon content.

- Individuals with disabilities are still woefully undervalued in our society.
- We waste too many of our resources testing, sorting, and labeling people, usually so we can justify serving, separating, or excluding them.
- The general education classroom (with individually appropriate supports) should be the first placement option for children with disabilities; separate special education schools and classes continue to be unnecessarily overused.
- Inclusive education is desirable; therefore, our efforts should be geared toward finding ways to make it work effectively for increasing numbers of students.
- People of all ages, with and without disabilities, have much to learn from each other.
- Collaborative teamwork is an important element of quality education.
- Families are the cornerstone of ongoing educational planning.

- Establishing a partnership between families and school personnel is vital to quality education.
- Competent general educators can effectively teach students with disabilities when provided with appropriate supports.
- Special educators and related service providers (e.g., physical therapists, occupational therapists, speech-language pathologists, school psychologists) can, and do, make important contributions for many students with special educational needs.
- Paraprofessionals are playing an increasingly prominent role in the education of students with disabilities. These hard-working folks typically are underpaid, undertrained, and undersupervised. Too often this means that they inappropriately become the de facto teacher for students with the most complex and challenging educational needs.
- All school personnel need to work under conditions that allow them to provide appropriate education for their students (e.g., adequate staff development and inservice education; supportive supervision; reasonable caseload sizes).
- The IEP (Individual Education Plan) can be a powerful and useful tool to facilitate quality education for students with disabilities. Unfortunately, too often it is misused.
- At the heart of a quality education are the relationships among the members of the educational community, the quality of the curriculum, and the integrity of the instruction. We must attend to all three components if we hope to assist students in experiencing valued life outcomes.

So as you read the cartoons, keep in mind that they are meant to encourage better educational practices by highlighting various absurdities of some of our current practices. I hope the cartoons stimulate you to think about things differently and that you find creative ways to use them in your own efforts to improve education for children and youth. I also hope that some of these cartoons make you smile and laugh, because we sure can use more of that in education.

Enjoy!

Michael F. Giangreco

Acknowledgments

Thanks to my colleagues and friends who inspired some of these cartoons: Linda Backus, Sister Elizabeth Candon, Ted Carr, Eileen CichoskiKelly, Mary Beth Doyle, Michael Hock, Tim Knoster, Joseph Lockavitch, Cathy Quinn, Dan Wilkins, and many Icelandic friends and colleagues. My greatest encouragement and many helpful suggestions came from my fun and funny family, my wife, Mary Beth, and my children, Melanie and Dan.

METHOD TO THE MADNESS:
UNBEKNOWNST TO HIS LEARNED COLLEAGUES, DR.G. GOT MORE PEOPLE TALKING ABOUT IMPORTANT ISSUES WHEN THEY WERE CLEVERLY DISGUISED AS CORNY CARTOONS.

THE LONE RANGER OF TEAMWORK:
A TEAM OF ONE GETS LITTLE DONE.

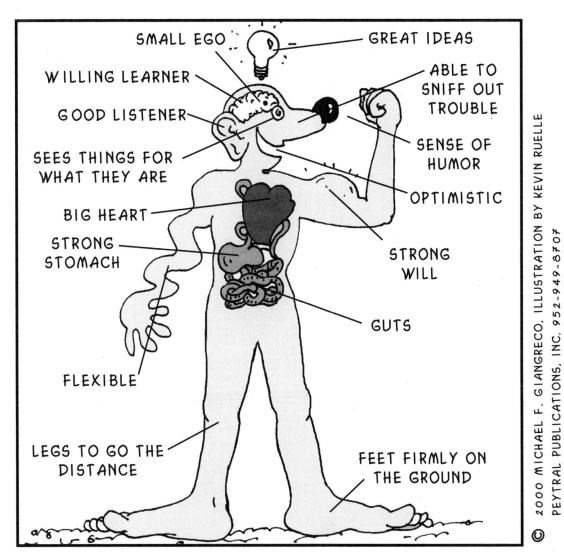

SMALL EGO

GREAT IDEAS

WILLING LEARNER

ABLE TO SNIFF OUT TROUBLE

GOOD LISTENER

SENSE OF HUMOR

SEES THINGS FOR WHAT THEY ARE

OPTIMISTIC

BIG HEART

STRONG STOMACH

STRONG WILL

GUTS

FLEXIBLE

LEGS TO GO THE DISTANCE

FEET FIRMLY ON THE GROUND

ANATOMY OF AN EFFECTIVE TEAM MEMBER

BUILDING BLOCKS OF
TEAMWORK

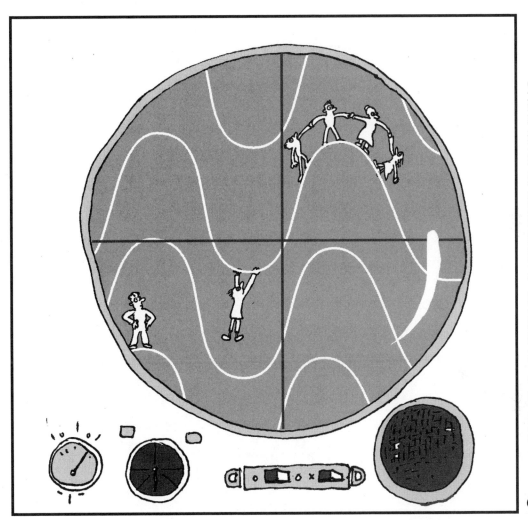

TEAM EFFECTIVENESS REQUIRES
ALL THE MEMBERS TO GET ON
THE SAME WAVELENGTH.

DISABILITY MYTHS SPAWN
COLLABORATION MYTHS.

SEVEN HABITS OF
COMPLETELY INEFFECTIVE
TEAM MEMBERS

CONSUMERS ENCOUNTER STAFF WITH
REASONABLE AFFECTIVE DISORDER.

KNOWING HOW HARD IT IS TO EFFECT
MEANINGFUL CHANGE IN PEOPLE,
MR. MOODY DECIDES TO
WORK HIS WAY UP TO IT BY
TEACHING OLD LOGS NEW TRICKS.

WITHOUT A VISION CONFUSION REIGNS!

THE TREADMILL OF CHANGE

UNLESS YOU HAVE THE SKILLS,
IT'S HIGH ANXIETY.

FANNING THE FLAMES OF CHANGE:
LIGHTING A FIRE UNDER PEOPLE WITHOUT
BURNING YOUR BRIDGES

TO ADDRESS THE LINGERING STIGMA OF
DISABILITY LABELING, MR. MOODY
IMPLEMENTS THE DISTRICT'S NEW
"STUDENT RELOCATION PROGRAM."

GREAT MOMENTS IN SPECIAL
EDUCATION HISTORY:
THE *1970'S* PROVIDE PROOF-POSITIVE
THAT DISABILITY IS
A SOCIAL CONSTRUCTION.

VEGAS CASINOS BUCKLE UNDER
POLITICAL PRESSURE TO STOP
STEREOTYPING DISABILITY
CHARACTERISTICS AS CRIMINAL BY
INVENTING THE TWO-ARMED BANDIT.

COUNTER INTELLIGENCE

17

DIAGNOSIS DU JOUR

MRS. SMITH ALWAYS LOOKS FOR POSITIVE WAYS TO DESCRIBE THE UNIQUENESS OF EACH STUDENT.

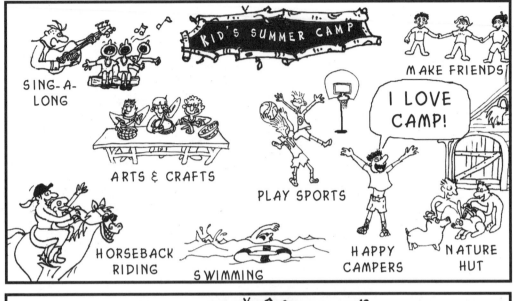

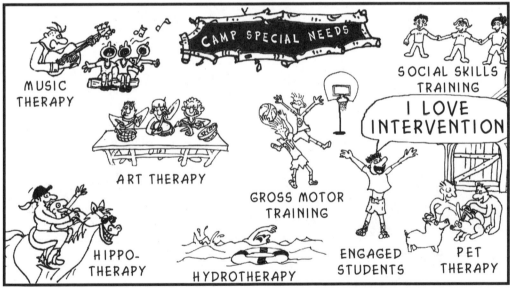

© 2000 MICHAEL F. GIANGRECO. ILLUSTRATION BY KEVIN RUELLE
PEYTRAL PUBLICATIONS, INC. 952-949-8707

DISABILITY LINGO
GOES TO CAMP!

WHAT DO YOU CHOOSE TO SEE?
WEEDS OR WILDFLOWERS?

© 2000 MICHAEL F. GIANGRECO. ILLUSTRATION BY KEVIN RUELLE
PEYTRAL PUBLICATIONS, INC. 952-949-8707

PROSPECTIVE TEACHERS OF THE FUTURE WILL NEED TO PASS THIS CRUCIAL TEST.

PROSPECTIVE EMPLOYEES GO THROUGH
A TRIAL BY FIRE TO HELP DETERMINE
THEIR SUITABILITY FOR THE
REALITIES OF PUBLIC SCHOOL.

UNEMPLOYED ACTORS ARE RECRUITED
TO FILL THE NATIONAL
TEACHER SHORTAGE.

WHAT HAPPENS WHEN PERSONNEL
AVAILABILITY AND MONEY GET TIGHT

WHO WILL WANT TO DO THESE JOBS
WHEN THEY GROW UP?

EMERGENCY TEACHER CERTIFICATION
WAIVER CLINIC

DRESS CODE.

MR. MOODY ENACTS A NEW POLICY:
"ALL FACULTY SHALL WEAR CLOTHING
CONSISTENT WITH THE ERA
THAT MATCHES THEIR
EDUCATIONAL PRACTICES."

STOMPING OUT THE CONDITIONS THAT
LEAD TO THE 3 BAD Rs:
RETENTION, REFERRAL, AND REJECTION

SCHOOLS ADOPT CONSUMER
EVALUATION TECHNIQUES
FROM INDUSTRY.

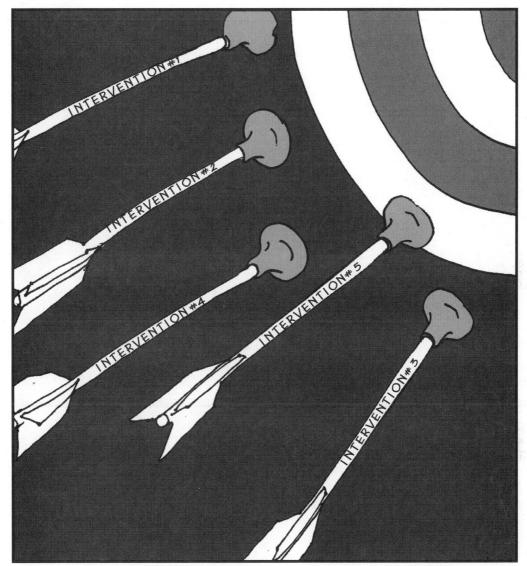

SHOOTING IN THE DARK:
WHAT HAPPENS WHEN YOU SELECT INTERVENTIONS WITHOUT GOOD ASSESSMENT DATA

REMEMBER,
THIS IS ONLY A TEST!

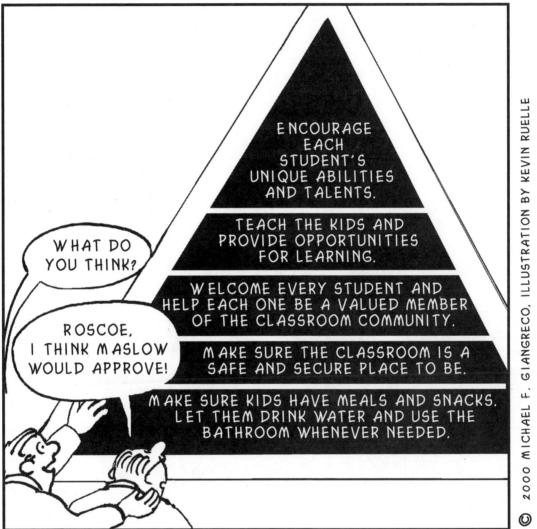

ROSCOE'S
HIERARCHY OF DEEDS

STAGES OF
CAREER
DEVELOPMENT

HOW PROFESSIONALS RESPOND TO
RULES THAT DON'T MAKE SENSE.

MRS. JONES EXPRESSES HER CONCERN ABOUT THE OBJECTIVE: "*DURING A VARIETY OF ACTIVITIES, DAVEY WILL DEMONSTRATE SUSTAINED SILENT BREATHING 100% OF THE TIME.*"

© 2000 MICHAEL F. GIANGRECO. ILLUSTRATION BY KEVIN RUELLE
PEYTRAL PUBLICATIONS, INC. 952-949-8707

MARY BETH'S SECRET WISH IS SHARED
BY PARENTS THE WORLD OVER.

SAM'S TEACHER IS DIAGNOSED WITH A
"TEACHING SPECTRUM DISORDER."

HARRY IS DIAGNOSED WITH
HARDENING OF THE ATTITUDES.

SCHOOL ADMINISTRATORS OFTEN FIND
THEMSELVES BETWEEN
A ROCK AND A HARD PLACE.

HOW MANY STUDENTS ARE FALLING
THROUGH THE CRACKS?

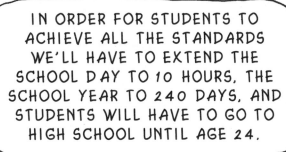

SCHOOL OFFICIALS PONDER
THEIR OPTIONS:
ADJUST THE STANDARDS,
ADJUST THE SCHOOL PROGRAM, OR
ADJUST BOTH.

STANDARDS ARE ADJUSTED AFTER THE
LEGISLATURE CONSIDERS A BILL
REQUIRING SCHOOL BOARD MEMBERS TO
PASS THE SAME ASSESSMENTS
GIVEN TO STUDENTS.

DESPERATE MEASURES

RAISING THE BAR
HAS A CHANCE ONLY WHEN
CURRICULUM, ASSESSMENT, AND
INSTRUCTION ARE ALIGNED.

IT'S A BALANCING ACT!

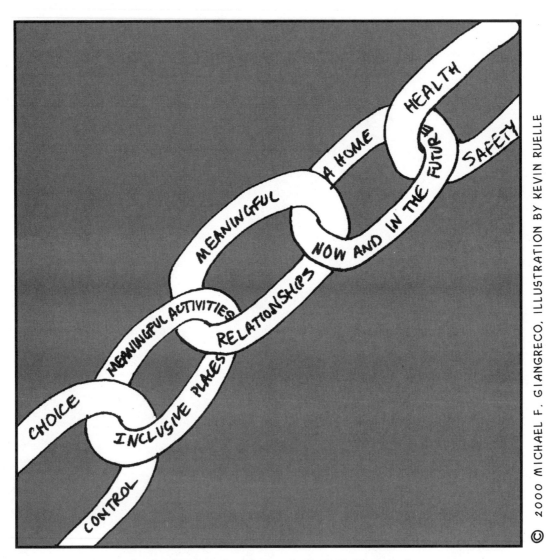

VALUED LIFE OUTCOMES:
SEEKING TO MAKE EVERY LINK STRONG.

FOLLOWING FIERCE FIGURING AND
FORMULATING, FERN FINDS THE COMMON
DENOMINATOR OF QUALITY EDUCATION.

IT'S A JUNGLE OUT THERE!

THE REAL KEY TO
SUCCESSFUL INSERVICE TRAINING

DO AS I SAY! NOT AS I DO!

UNIVERSITY PROMOTION MISHAP #3:

NEW SCHOLARSHIP
MEETS OLD SCHOLARS.

© 2000 MICHAEL F. GIANGRECO. ILLUSTRATION BY KEVIN RUELLE
PEYTRAL PUBLICATIONS, INC. 952-949-8707

FAULTY RESEARCH LOGIC

WHATEVER HYPE IS SERVED UP,
TAKE IT WITH *AT LEAST*
A GRAIN OF SALT.

DON'T BE SEDUCED!
JUST BECAUSE IT LOOKS GOOD AT FIRST
GLANCE DOESN'T MEAN IT'S THE RIGHT
SOLUTION.

LEGISLATIVE PRACTICAL JOKES

WARNING!
This is a nun's car. If you steal it, you may as well drive straight to hell.

God Bless You.

AFTER A RECENT THEFT, FRED POSTS A WARNING FOR THOSE WHO MAY NOT HAVE HAD THE BENEFIT OF CHARACTER EDUCATION.

WIDE ACCEPTANCE-
SHORT, CLEAR, CONCISE

CONSIDERED TOO
SARCASTIC BY SOME

LEADS TO MANY QUESTIONS
PEOPLE CAN'T ANSWER

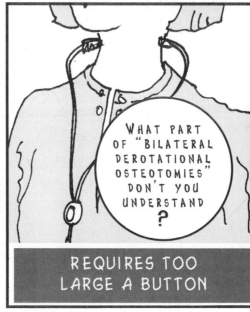

REQUIRES TOO
LARGE A BUTTON

WHY SPIN-OFF SLOGANS ARE NEVER AS GOOD AS THE ORIGINAL

AFTER RECEIVING INEVITABLE NEWS,
YOU COULD HEAR A CHIN DROP.

MR. MOODY CONTINUES TO BE BEFUDDLED
BY THE LACK OF CLEAR DEFINITIONS.

OPENING THE DOOR ON
SPECIAL CLASS EUPHEMISMS

NO DUMPING!

DON'T MISS THE BOAT!

DOUBLE STANDARD # 5:
IF IT'S NOT OK TO DISRUPT THE
EDUCATION OF STUDENTS *WITHOUT*
DISABILITIES, WHY IS IT OK TO DISRUPT
THE EDUCATION OF
STUDENTS *WITH* DISABILITIES?

AVOID THE TRAPS OF QUASI-INCLUSION:
DON'T TAKE THE BAIT!

ANSWERING QUESTIONS WITH QUESTIONS

BOLDLY NOT GOING WHERE TOO MANY
OTHERS HAVE GONE BEFORE!

WHEN IT COMES TO ENFORCING *IDEA*,
THE LONG ARM OF THE LAW
ISN'T LONG ENOUGH.

RITA RETURNS TO DIG UP THE
ROOTS OF SPECIAL EDUCATION.

THE AMAZING
SPECIAL EDUCATION MAIZE

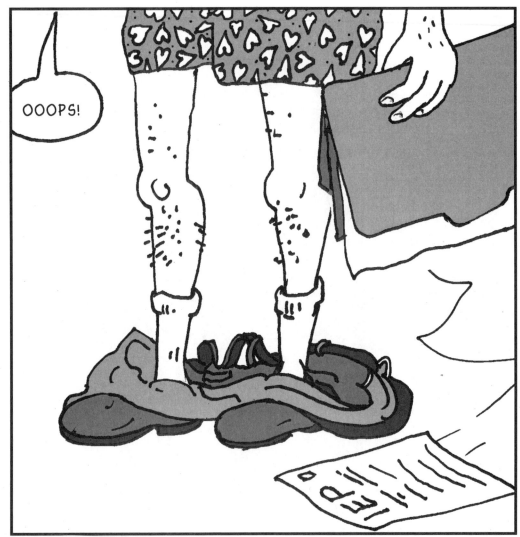

ARE YOU PREPARED
FOR *ALL* YOUR STUDENTS?
DON'T BE
CAUGHT WITH YOUR PANTS DOWN!

TEAMMATES ENGAGE IN THEIR ANNUAL
POST-IEP COMPLETION RITUAL.

HARVEY FOLLOWS THE COACH ON THE
PATH TOWARD INCLUSIONVILLE.

THE THREE FACES OF BEAV

LABORATORY RETRIEVER

SIMPLE ACCOMMODATIONS
IN THE AGE OF LITIGATION

THEATRE OF THE ABSURD

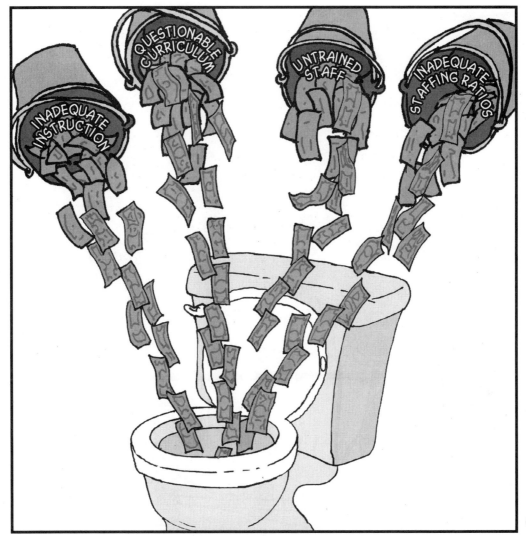

UNLESS YOU SPEND ENOUGH MONEY
TO MEET A BASIC
THRESHOLD OF EFFECTIVENESS,
YOU MIGHT AS WELL JUST FLUSH IT!

HOW MUCH CAKE CAN ONE PERSON EAT?

IF YOUR CASELOAD IS TOO BIG, YOU ARE
SKATING ON THIN ICE.

PRACTICE PREVENTING PROBLEMS:
FIND OUT WHAT THE LAST STRAW WILL
BE BEFORE IT'S TOO LATE.

SHOPPING AROUND:
DO YOU KNOW THESE PEOPLE?
THEY NEVER MET A THERAPY
THEY DIDN'T LIKE.

THE OLD MEDICAL MODEL

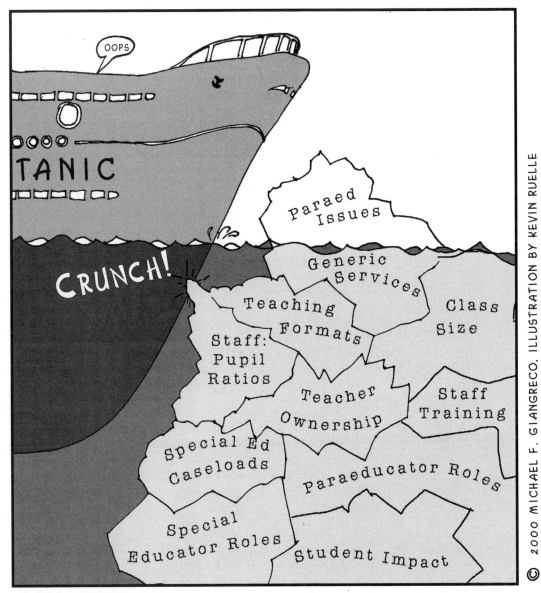

PARAEDUCATOR ISSUES:
JUST THE TIP OF THE ICEBERG

BAND-AID APPROACH:
ARE WE EXPECTING TOO MUCH
OF INSTRUCTIONAL ASSISTANTS?

WHAT'S WRONG WITH THIS PICTURE?

IF YOU NEED STAFF WITH THE SKILLS OF TEACHERS AND SPECIAL EDUCATORS, MAYBE YOU NEED TO HIRE TEACHERS AND SPECIAL EDUCATORS.

CLASSROOM ASSISTANTS:
EXPECT AN EXTRA PAIR OF
HELPING HANDS. THE OTHER GREAT
THINGS THEY DO ARE GRAVY.

HAVING BEEN A PARAEDUCATOR FOR A COUPLE OF YEARS, DOROTHY KNEW THAT THE FINAL CLAUSE COULD MEAN JUST ABOUT ANYTHING.

DECISIONS ABOUT A CHILD'S LIFE:
SOMEONE IN THE *FAMILY* SHOULD BE
WEARING THE PANTS.

WORD PROBLEMS

SCHOOL STAFF FIND IT
CHALLENGING TO DEVELOP A
COHERENT BEHAVIOR PLAN WHEN
THEIR PRACTICES ARE REFLECTIVE
OF DIFFERENT VALUES AND ERAS.

EXPERTS GET BIG BUCKS
FOR CONSULTATION TO REMIND
FOLKS THAT "INTERVENTION"
CAN BE EFFECTIVE ONLY
BEFORE A CRISIS OCCURS.

LITTLE SHOP OF HORRORS

ODD JOBS!

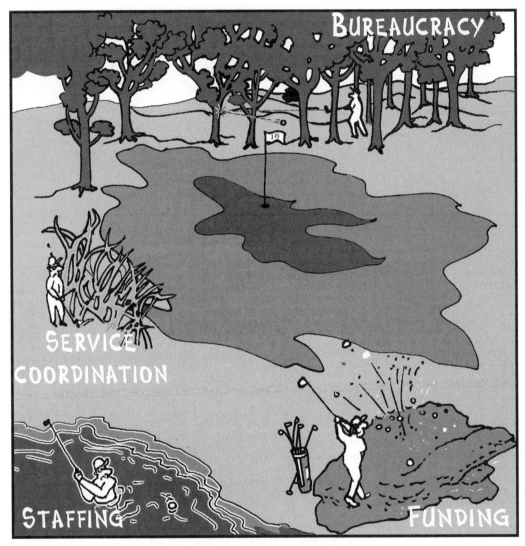

THE HAZARDS
OF TRANSITION PLANNING
ARE PAR FOR THE COURSE.

SUPPORTED EMPLOYMENT LESSON # 6:
GIVE A PERSON A FISH AND THAT
PERSON EATS FOR A DAY. TEACH A
PERSON TO *WORK* AND THAT PERSON
CAN BUY A FISH ANY DAY!

JUDY'S BRAND OF
"IN-YOUR-FACE"
SELF-ADVOCACY FIRST SHOWED
ITSELF AT AN EARLY AGE.

PETER PONDERS OVER APPAREL TO WEAR
TO HIS NEXT IEP MEETING.

© 2000 MICHAEL F. GIANGRECO. ILLUSTRATION BY KEVIN RUELLE
PEYTRAL PUBLICATIONS, INC. 952-949-8707

INSPIRED BY DAN WILKINS

RODNEY'S SELF-ADVOCACY TAKES ON A DECIDEDLY INTERNATIONAL FLAIR.

CLEARING A PATH
FOR PEOPLE WITH SPECIAL NEEDS
CLEARS THE PATH FOR EVERYONE!

Additional Cartoons!
Written by Michael F. Giangreco and Illustrated by Kevin Ruelle

With wit, humor and profound one-liners, Michael Giangreco and Kevin Ruelle will transform your thinking as you take a lighter look at the often comical and occasionally harsh truth in the ever-changing field of special education.

These cartoon books, shed light onto the real-life situations frequently encountered by those involved with the special education system. Each of the following publications include a collection of 100+ carefully crafted cartoons that will inspire and entertain, while providing a scrupulous look into the absurdities and realities of virtually all areas of special education.

Each publication includes a wide range of topics: inclusive education, self-advocacy, paraprofessionals, families, positive behavior support, support services, least restrictive environment, collaboration, individual education plans, disability labeling, and standards are only a few.

These cartoons are on exceptional staff development tool as the full-page cartoons may be reproduced as transparencies. Use the cartoons to help inform, encourage dialogue, spur action to improve education, and reduce stress through laughter.

Ants in His Pants:
Absurdities and Realities of Special Education 1998

Flying by the Seat of Your Pants:
More Absurdities and Realities of Special Education 1999

Teaching Old Logs New Tricks:
More Absurdities and Realities of Education 2000

If you would like additional information about these books please call toll free 1-877-739-8725. We will be happy to help you.

If you have questions, would like to request a catalog, or place an order, please contact Peytral Publications, Inc. We will be happy to help you.

Peytral Publications, Inc.
PO Box 1162
Minnetonka, MN 55345

Toll free orders: 1-877-PEYTRAL (877-739-8725)
Questions: (952) 949-8707
Fax: 952.906.9777

Or visit us online at:
www.peytral.com